RUGS OF THE CAUCASUS

ORGANIZED BY

JAMES VERBRUGGE
AND DALE COUCH

GEORGIA MUSEUM OF ART, UNIVERSITY OF GEORGIA
JANUARY 30 – APRIL 27, 2014

© 2014 Georgia Museum of Art, University of Georgia

Published by the Georgia Museum of Art, University of Georgia. All rights reserved. No part of this book may be reproduced without the written consent of the publishers.

Printed in an edition of 1,000 by Four Colour Imports, Ltd.

Design: **Scott Sosebee**
Department of Publications: **Hillary Brown**
Publications Interns: **Kate Douds** and **Elizabeth Fontaine**

Library of Congress Cataloging-in-Publication Data

Rugs of the Caucasus / organized by James Verbrugge and Dale Couch.
    pages cm
"Georgia Museum of Art, University of Georgia, January 30/April 27, 2014."
Includes bibliographical references.
ISBN-13: 978-0-915977-84-0 (alk. paper)
ISBN-10: 0-915977-84-2 (alk. paper)
1. Rugs, Caucasian--Private collections--United States--Exhibitions. 2. Verbrugge, James A.--Art collections--Exhibitions. I. Verbrugge, James A. Nineteenth-century treasures from the Caucasus. II. Georgia Museum of Art.
NK2809.C3R84 2014
746.7'5907475818--dc23
                    2013045942

Partial support for the exhibitions and programs at the Georgia Museum of Art is provided by the W. Newton Morris Charitable Foundation and the Friends of the Georgia Museum of Art. Individuals, foundations, and corporations provide additional support through their gifts to the University of Georgia Foundation.

TABLE OF CONTENTS

Foreword 4

Nineteenth-Century Treasures from the Caucasus:
An Educational Journey 7

Catalogue of the Exhibition 21

    Dated Kuba Soumack rug, East Caucasus 23

    Dated Daghestan prayer rug, East Caucasus, Azerbaijan 25

    Dated Kazak rug, West Caucasus, Armenia 27

    Dated Kazak prayer rug, West Caucasus, Armenia 29

    Dated Shirvan prayer rug, East Caucasus, Azerbaijan 31

    Eagle Soumack rug, Cheleberd design Karabagh 33

    Moghan rug, Plains of Southeast Caucasus, Azerbaijan 35

    Moghan rug, Plains of Southeast Caucasus, Azerbaijan 37

    Moghan rug, Plains of Southeast Caucasus, Azerbaijan 39

    Sewan Kazak rug, West Caucasus, Armenia 41

    Qashqai rug, Southwest Persia 43

A Note on the Mounts 46

FOREWORD

A powerful and succinct statement is made when a few objects of elevated quality carefully selected create a small exhibition that effectively tells a big story. Nineteenth-century rugs of the Caucasus have fascinated American and European collectors throughout the past century. Indeed, Western societies were consumers of these rugs during much of the nineteenth and early twentieth centuries. Within the United States, the South displayed a notable preference for Persian rugs, but Caucasian examples were found here as well. In fact, an advertisement in the *Milledgeville News* (July 2, 1909) specifically mentions "one Kajac rug 3 feet 6 by 4 feet 4 inches, was $16.00; now $12.00." Clearly, the informed reader was expected to recognize the tribal name. Caucasian rugs were so common in American and European households that today they seem as familiar as they do exotic. Caucasian rugs of varying quality and condition have long been a staple at American estate sales.

Western use of "oriental" rugs often left them on hard floors at entryways and other points of heavy foot traffic, meaning they were used harshly for decades. Most of them lost their rich pile, and many became threadbare. Even so, they retain a muted elegance and a form of patina often cherished by later collectors. Pleasing as these aged objects now are, they are visually far removed from the rugs valued in the land of their manufacture, where they were gently used and treasured. These latter examples retain thick pile and rich colors that astound even the trained Western eye. They gleam with an intense beauty and luster unrecoverable by the lovely worn examples from American homes. This less harsh aging leads to the term "Armenian wear," meaning less wear. It is left to the brilliant survivals of "Armenian wear" to tell the true story of this wonderful rug art.

It is remarkable that the Verbrugge collection consists of magnificent rugs in sterling condition; it is astonishing that so many of them are dated. From 1805 on, these stellar dated examples of the rug weavers' art span the century they represent. These choice rugs present the story of a rich tradition as it unfolded in Western Asia and revive the image our ancestors viewed when they first purchased these intricate textiles.

The embedded chronology allows this collection to speak to design evolution as well as quality.

The creation and love of beauty is an affirmation of life. Collecting art manifests this reality. The Verbrugge collection, meaningfully,

CAUCASIAN RUGS were so common in American and European households that today they seem as familiar as they do exotic.

began after deep personal loss for Jim and Marcia Verbrugge. Athens is fortunate to be home to this couple, this connoisseur, and this collection. We dedicate this show to their late son Jason Mark Verbrugge.

Dale Couch
Curator of Decorative Arts
Georgia Museum of Art

This exhibition was designed and installed by **David Foster Chamberlain**

NINETEENTH-CENTURY TREASURES FROM THE CAUCASUS:
An Educational Journey

JAMES A. VERBRUGGE

INTRODUCTION:
The Geographical, Historical, and Cultural Context

The region known as the Caucasus consists of the contemporary countries of Armenia, Azerbaijan, and Georgia, among others. Although geographically included in the region, the Republics of Daghestan and Chechnya are part of the Russian Federation. This broadly defined area is bounded by the Black Sea on the west and the Caspian Sea on the east, with Russia to the north, Iran to the south, and Turkey to the west. A point that divides Europe from Asia, it has a long history of confrontations between Christianity and Islam.[1] The countries of the southern Caucasus have been a center of rug production for centuries, principally the countries of Armenia and Azerbaijan. This region borders on Turkey to the west and Iran to the south, both of which also have long traditions of rug weaving.

Armenia especially has experienced political and religious unrest for hundreds of years, partially due to its being the first country to adopt Christianity as the official state religion, in 301 CE.[2] Over succeeding centuries, Islam became the dominant religion in surrounding countries, and Armenians became a religious minority, resulting in considerable tension between Armenia and, especially, Turkey during the period of the Ottoman Empire. Devastating violence resulted against the Armenian settlements in both Armenia and the Armenian-populated sections of Turkey. The chaos and violence over the years led to the scattering of the Armenian people across the Caucasus. Such migrations can be traced as far back as 1,700 years, but for our purposes those from the nineteenth and twentieth centuries are the most important.

The first modern addition to this diaspora occurred in the 1890s during and following the Hamidian Massacre, when hundreds of thousands of Armenians residing in the Ottoman Empire were persecuted and killed. The second, and perhaps the most famous, took place between 1915 and 1920 during and following the Armenian Genocide in which between 1 million and 1.5 million Armenians living in Turkey and in Armenia were killed. The third occurred following World War II, when Armenians who earlier had been forced south into countries of the Middle East faced increasing religious and ethnic hostilities, resulting in an exodus to the West. In each of these three instances, Armenians were persecuted and forced into labor or killed as non-Muslim infidels.

Armenians preferred the northeastern United States in the early twentieth century and southern California between 1989 and the early 1990s.[3]

For centuries, Armenia and Azerbaijan have been centers of rug and textile weaving. The earliest known surviving rug, the Pazyryk carpet, which dates to the fifth century BCE, has often been attributed to early Armenians. The nineteenth century is often

THE EARLIEST known surviving rug, the Pazyryk carpet, which dates to the fifth century BCE, has often been attributed to early Armenians.

The most recent large-scale Armenian migration occurred from 1989 to the early 1990s, following the demise of the Soviet Union. All countries in the Caucasus region had been a part of the U.S.S.R. and had subsumed their individual identities into the collective. When the wall collapsed, people had the opportunity to leave the region voluntarily and emigrate to the West, often the United States.

viewed as the apex of rug-weaving culture in the Caucasus, although there are some surviving examples of sixteenth-, seventeenth-, and eighteenth-century rugs. Women wove most nineteenth-century rugs from the Caucasus in homes and villages as a way of making a living for themselves and their families. This means of production stands in sharp contrast to the more controlled commercial environment in which many Persian rugs were woven in the urban centers of Iran, such as Istfahan or Kashan. Nineteenth-century Persian rugs referred to as "tribal" or "nomadic" derived from rural areas. During the 1890s, when Armenia and Azerbaijan were part of the Russian Federation, its central authorities attempted to reinvigorate rug production for export, including the fabrication of large quantities of organic dyes, which were then provided to local weavers as a way of mitigating the use of inorganic dyes that had come into use.[4] In the 1920s, the Soviet Union took over the region and almost completely centralized control of rug production. Rug weaving as an art form then deteriorated in quality, as manifested in what came to be known as five-year-plan rugs between 1927 and 1932.

RUGS INCLUDED IN THE EXHIBITION

It is within this volatile cultural and political context that one must view rugs from the Caucasus. Each of the rugs in this exhibition originated from a specific area of the region. In some cases, one can identify the specific village where a rug was woven. Some can also be traced with a high degree of certainty to one of the more recent migrations from Armenia. I selected these specific rugs to present a comparative analysis of nineteenth-century rugs from the Caucasus both over time and across types. Other issues include dates in rugs and their alternative renderings, the designs and construction of rugs, and alternative portrayals of basic designs in a specific subtype of rug. The rugs in the exhibition span nearly the entire nineteenth century, with the earliest rug from 1805 and the latest from the 1880s, thereby offering the opportunity to make a variety of comparisons over a roughly eighty-year period.

Dates in rugs have long been a subject of controversy, regularly questioned as to their authenticity. Incorrect dates or alterations to dates are two of the most common concerns of collectors and experts; however, without strong evidence to the contrary, there is no reason to doubt the reliability of the dates for the five rugs in the exhibition that have them.[5] Few rugs dated before 1800 have survived, so it is important to note that the two in the exhibition from the very early 1800s are highly unusual and significant.

Catalogue number 3 is the only one of the five in which the year of its weaving, 1849, is displayed

> **EACH OF THE RUGS** in this exhibition originated from a specific area of the region. In some cases, one can identify the specific village where a rug was woven.

according to the Christian or Gregorian calendar, suggesting a Christian rather than a Muslim weaver. The other four dated rugs (cat. nos. 1, 2, 4, and 5) are rendered with Arabic numerals according to the Islamic calendar, with dates that convert to 1805, 1815, 1878, and 1886 in the Gregorian calendar. The first year in the Islamic calendar represents the beginning of the pilgrimage of the prophet Mohammed from Mecca to Medina in 622 CE. To arrive at a rough approximation of the Gregorian date, one must take into account both the difference in the calendar start dates and the fact that the Islamic calendar is a lunar one.[6]

The cross-section of rugs from the nineteenth century in this exhibition enables several types of comparisons. First, one can look at the evolution of rug design during the nineteenth century. Catalogue number 2, which dates from 1805 / 1815, is a very early Daghestan prayer rug; number 5 is a Shirvan prayer rug dated some seventy years later (1886). In many ways, the similarities between these two rugs outweigh their differences. The minor borders that flank the major border in each and surround the *mihrab* (prayer niche) include a version of the so-called "crosses and sevens" design. A nearly identical "sawtooth" minor border is similarly located in each. Both employ a repeating design in the field that exhibits great variety in individual forms, and both display a large number of colors throughout, understandably considerably more vivid in the later rug. Besides the different major borders (dragon design in the white field, leaf and calyx in the blue field), one observes two other differences. The field design in the Daghestan rug consists of flowers and that of the Shirvan rug of botehs with additional tertiary ornaments including fanciful birds. Finally, the wonderful uncluttered spacing and the naturalistic drawing in the Daghestan rug distinguish it from its younger counterpart from Shirvan.[7]

Catalogue number 4 is an excellent example of a dated Kazak prayer rug in a prayer design distinctly different from that of catalogue numbers 2 and 5. The challenge with Kazak prayer rugs is to attribute their origin to a specific village in the Caucasus. Although Fachralo and Borjalou Kazak prayer rugs are plentiful, few published examples exist with the specific rendering of the mihrab portrayed in catalogue number 4.[8] In this case, the design of the prayer arch forms an inner field, which then floats on an open brick-red field. Derivations of the three major ornaments in the blue field can be found in non-prayer Karachopt Kazaks, which suggests one possible village origin.[9] The sloping shoulders of the mihrab and the re-entrant feature at the bottom of the field relate to some old Turkish prayer rugs.

A second comparison can result from examining the construction of the various weavings. Catalogue numbers 1 and 6 were woven using a soumack technique, and the others employ a knotted-pile method. The flat-stitched soumack offers the clearest, most defined way to render design, whereas knotted-pile weaving, which is thicker, portrays color to its best advantage. Catalogue number 6 is unusual because its design most often is produced in knotted pile. Catalogue number 1 is not only the oldest dated rug in the exhibition, but arguably the most colorful, countering the prevalent idea that piled rugs show the best color. Most authorities believe that vegetable (natural) color technology degraded during the course of the nineteenth century, and the early date of this rug, with its exquisite color, bolsters that notion. It is also unusual to see a rug from the Caucasus woven in two separate pieces on a narrow loom, as here, then sewn together. One can only speculate about why. Did the village weaver not have a loom of sufficient width? Or might it have been made by nomadic weavers who, because of their migratory nature, used narrow looms because they were easier to transport?

Third, the collection presents a small variety of the different categories of rugs from the Caucasus, some far more unusual than others. The general rule is that rugs from the region are named for the geographic area or village in which they were woven. Catalogue number 1 was produced in Kuba in northeast Azerbaijan

CATALOGUE NUMBER 1 is not only the oldest dated rug in the exhibition, but arguably the most colorful, countering the prevalent idea that piled rugs show the best color.

whereas catalogue number 3 was made in Kazak, which is in Armenia in the western Caucasus. In addition to its early date, this latter rug retains the full pile of its original weave, despite some evidence of wear. Catalogue number 6, commonly called an "eagle Kazak," was actually produced in Karabagh, a Christian Armenian enclave within predominantly Islamic Azerbaijan.

Catalogue number 10 is among the most recognizable rug types from the Caucasus and is the most easily identified in the exhibition as an Armenian rug. It is a Sewan Kazak, a form that has a large cruciform medallion as the dominant feature. The cruciform or Armenian cross may represent an Armenian church. Peter Stone suggests that crosses have been a design field of many cultures and do not necessarily show Christian religious significance.[10] Woven in the Lake Sewan area of Armenia, this example features the dark blue cruciform on a red field with a squared hexagon end (sometimes an arrowhead in other examples). In its full pile condition, it is a wonderful example of a rug dating from the fourth quarter of the nineteenth century that is Armenian-aged rather than American-aged as it almost certainly left the country only after the collapse of the Soviet Union.[11]

James Opie briefly discusses catalogue number 11, a very important and highly regarded textile, elsewhere in this volume. This rug is actually from the category of rugs known as Qashqais, from southwest Persia, but it has design similarities with rugs from the Caucasus. In this case, the inner field (field-within-a-field) has latch-hook diamond medallions, which also appear on a number of rugs from the Caucasus, a comparison that suggests the possible migration of designs between disparate groups across regions.

The exhibition also includes three examples of the rug type known as Moghan that date from the third quarter of the nineteenth century. This type originates from the plains of the Southeast Caucasus in Azerbaijan. The principal design feature of the Moghan is the Memling gul, named for the well-known fifteenth-century Flemish painter Hans Memling. In some of his work (e.g., *The Virgin and Child Between Saint James and Saint Dominic*, ca. 1490, Musée du Louvre), he used a rug in which the primary ornament was the gul as background in the painting. A "gul" ("flower" in Persian) is basically an octagonal or angular medallion, often repeated to form an all-over pattern in the field. Catalogue number 7 serves as a wonderful illustration of the Moghan format, with three distinct and separable columns of six guls. The guls appear to float separately from one another due to the diamond-shaped secondary ornaments, which create visual space between the guls. Although the field of guls is the most obvious feature, the structure and spacing of the individual guls create secondary viewing fields.

Catalogue number 8 portrays the Memling guls in a tightly clustered format with virtually no separation. The result is a vivid display of colors on a bed of twenty-one interconnected octagonal lattices.[12] In rather sharp contrast, catalogue number 9 offers a different and more primitive rendering of the Memling gul. Indeed, the guls almost become of secondary importance due to the presence of the large central medallion. The weaver seems to be telling a part of her life story with the medallion and its surrounding figures, which feature stylized human figures and creatures, with one of the latter being ridden by a bird. The muted colors in this example also set it apart from the two other Moghans. One can speculate that it may be not a Moghan, but an example of a weaver who picked up the Moghan format and added her own flair with the medallion.

This exhibition does not attempt to present all the main types

THE EXHIBITION also includes three examples of the rug type known as Moghan that date from the third quarter of the nineteenth century.

of rugs woven in the Caucasus during the nineteenth century, which would probably number between ten and fifteen, significantly more if one were to count the subtypes within each broad category.[13] Nor does it address the many issues that could be discussed about any collection or exhibition of rugs from the Caucasus.[14] It does display a series of striking and important rugs, including several rare examples of pre-1850 rugs, a very early soumack weave rug, and unusual and striking portrayals of the Memling gul group of rugs. In addition, it features one of the most famous rugs from outside the region, but one with characteristics that resemble those of rugs from the Caucasus. In so doing, the exhibition enables us to discuss several interesting aspects of nineteenth-century rugs from this historic and war-torn region.

James Verbrugge is professor of finance emeritus at the University of Georgia; over the years, he developed a passion for rugs from the Caucasus.

AUTHOR'S NOTE:

I am greatly indebted to Harold Myers of Seattle, Washington, for sharing his vast expertise in all things about antique rugs from this region as well as village and tribal rugs more generally. Myers is the proprietor of Oasis Rugs and some of the rugs in the exhibition were acquired from his dealership or through his connections. He is also a collector, specializing in eighteenth- and nineteenth-century Central Asian textiles. I would also like to acknowledge noted rug connoisseur and scholar James Opie, who provided specific comments on one of the rugs in the exhibition.

ENDNOTES

1 Because the region is bounded by so many geographic features and political entities, the Caucasus, especially the South Caucasus, has often been labeled the "lands in-between." Thomas de Waal, *The Caucasus: An Introduction* (Oxford: Oxford University Press, 2010); and Peter F. Stone, *The Oriental Rug Lexicon* (Seattle: University of Washington Press, 1997).

2 Mario Alexis Portella and Abba Abraham Buruk Woldegaber have recently challenged this claim in their book *Abyssinian Christianity: The First Christian Nation?* (Carpinteria, CA: BP Editing, 2012).

3 Although the southeastern United States was not one of the main areas to which Armenians migrated, several established rug dealerships in the Atlanta area, one of which (Sharian Rugs) survives and is now in its fourth generation of family ownership.

4 Other aspects of what was known as the Kustar' program (after the word for craftsperson) included training facilities, art schools, and overseas outlets. "Kustar' Program in Caucasia," Richard E. Wright Research Reports, 2009, http://richardewright.com/0906_kustar.html.

5 See, for example, Ian Bennett, *Oriental Rugs*, vol. 1, *Caucasian* (Woodbridge, Suffolk, England: Oriental Textile Press, 1981), 14–16; and Reinhard G. Hubel, *The Book of Carpets,* trans. Katherine Watson (London: Barrie & Jenkins, 1971), 314–16.

6 See Bennett (14–16) for a detailed discussion of the conversion method, plus a conversion table for the years 1178–1415 AH (Islamic calendar, with AH standing for anno Hegirae), which convert into the years 1764–1994 AD. Hubel (314–16) also extensively addresses the conversion method.

7 The classic work on prayer rugs from the Caucasus is Ralph Kaffel, *Caucasian Prayer Rugs* (London: Laurence King in conjunction with Hali Publications, 1998).

8 See Kaffel, plate 17.

9 Bennett, plate 34.

10 Stone, 58.

11 Dealers and collectors make distinctions between rugs aged in Armenia and those aged in the United States. Rugs made in the nineteenth century for export were most often used and, therefore, show evidence of wear. Those retained by the weaver or her customers in Armenia were highly prized and were often stored or hung on walls, thus retaining their full pile.

12 Based on the provenance of these rugs, there is strong evidence that catalogue numbers 4 and 7 came to the United States during or immediately following 1915–20.

13 Bennett, for example, lists seventeen subgroups under the broader category of Kazak.

14 In addition to the publications cited above, there are several other excellent and highly regarded books on the subject of rugs from the Caucasus. One of the earliest significant publications is Ulrich Schurmann, *Caucasian Rugs: A Detailed Presentation of the Art of Carpet Weaving in the Various Districts of the Caucasus During the 18th and 19th Century* (Braunschweig: Klinkhardt & Biermann, 1961). Others include James D. Burns, *The Caucasus: Traditions in Weaving* (Seattle: Court Street Press, 1987); Murray L. Eiland Jr. and Murray Eiland III, *Oriental Carpets: A Complete Guide*, 4th ed, (Boston: Little, Brown, 1998); John T. Wertime and Richard E. Wright, *Caucasian Carpets and Covers: The Weaving Culture* (London: Hali Publications, 1995); Walter A. Hawley, *Oriental Rugs: Antique and Modern* (New York: Dodd, Mead, 1921; reprinted numerous times); Joseph McMullan, *Islamic Carpets* (New York: Near Eastern Art Research Center, 1965); Raoul Tschebull, *Kazak Carpets of the Caucasus* (New York: Near Eastern Art Research Center, 1971); Charles Grant Ellis, *Early Caucasian Rugs* (Washington, DC: Textile Museum, 1975); Erwin Gans-Ruedin, *Caucasian Carpets* (New York, Rizzoli, 1986). Over the years, numerous articles on the subject have also been published in the highly acclaimed international journal on textiles, *Hali: The International Magazine of Antique Carpets and Textile Arts*, for example Viken Sassouni, "Armenian Church Floor Plans: A Hitherto Unidentified Design in Oriental Rugs," *Hali* 4, no. 1 (1981): 24–28; and Louise Shelley and Richard Wright, "Caucasian Rugs in the Late Nineteenth Century," *Hali* 3, no. 1 (1980): 3–7.

CATALOGUE OF THE EXHIBITION

All rugs collection of
James A. and **Marcia B. Verbrugge**.

1. **Dated Kuba Soumack rug, East Caucasus, 1805, with the date displayed based on the Islamic calendar as 1220**

   Wool-on-wool • 110 x 86 inches

Among the earliest known dated examples of this form, this textile also demonstrates the enormous color variety that captivates devotees of rugs from the Caucasus, with at least thirteen colors on the wool face. Uncommonly, it was woven in two separate pieces on a narrow loom, which may suggest nomadic weavers rather than village weavers.

2. Dated Daghestan prayer rug, East Caucasus, Azerbaijan, 1805/1815

Wool-on-wool • 58 x 46 inches

This early prayer rug is unusual in that it has two dates in the weaving: 1805 and 1815. The reason for the two dates is known only to the original early-nineteenth–century weaver. The rug does have damage from wear over two centuries, but restoration of such an early example is typically not undertaken. It is preferable to exhibit it in the form in which it now appears.

3. Dated Kazak rug, West Caucasus, Armenia, 1849 (Gregorian calendar)

Wool-on-wool • 92 x 60 inches

Dated rugs before 1850 are not common. The date's appearance in Gregorian calendar years may suggest a Christian rather than Muslim weaver. Despite some wear, this rug retains almost the full pile of its original weave, indicating careful use over its 160-year history.

4. Dated Kazak prayer rug, West Caucasus, Armenia, 1878

Wool-on-wool • 62 x 42 inches

This well-rendered Kazak prayer rug has exceptional color throughout and a blue mihrab with striking abrash (or mottling, resulting from color variation). The mihrab has an unusually large indent, and the rug has certain features commonly found in Karachoph Kazaks.

5. Dated Shirvan prayer rug, East Caucasus, Azerbaijan, 1886 (with date displayed based on Islamic calendar as 1304)

Wool-on-wool • 59 x 43 inches

This rug exhibits the exceptionally fine weave that is typical of the best Shirvan rugs. Its design features a yellow-ground depiction of the prayer niche (mihrab) and a blue/black field overall, covered artistically with botehs and a variety of animal, bird, and shrub motifs. Nearly at the end of the period of exceptional weave and color saturation, this rug maintains the tradition of high quality of color, design, and structure in the form.

6. Eagle Soumack rug, Cheleberd design, Karabagh, Azerbaijan, 3rd quarter, 19th century

Wool-on-wool • 117 x 69 inches

The "eagle" design of this rug is more commonly displayed on piled rugs than on soumack-weave rugs. In this format, the design and large number of colors take on a more dramatic, clearer, and more distinct portrayal than is generally the case for a rug constructed in the wool-pile format. The exceptionally fine weaving in soumacks has often been lost or badly damaged over a century and a half due to use and exposure, but not in this case.

7. Moghan rug, Plains of Southeast Caucasus, Azerbaijan, 3rd quarter, 19th century

Wool-on-wool • 89 x 66 inches

The principal design feature of the Moghan subclass of Caucasian rugs is the Memling gul, named for the well-known fifteenth-century Flemish painter Hans Memling. The dominant feature of this rug is the gul field, where the well-spaced guls appear to float separately from one another. The secondary ornaments are the large diamonds that separate guls and themselves contain numerous smaller diamonds, not all of which are alike. While the eye is initially drawn to the large guls, the array of smaller and larger diamonds forms a separate viewing field.

8. Moghan rug, Plains of Southeast Caucasus, Azerbaijan, 3rd quarter, 19th century

Wool-on-wool • 94 x 59 inches

The guls in this rug are almost completely attached to one another, with separation appearing almost incidental. The modest separation between the Memling guls with small diamonds, while colorful, almost disappears as even a secondary field. Whether this tendency toward connecting the guls rather than more generous spacing indicates an evolution of the Moghan design or simply the weaver's choice is unclear.

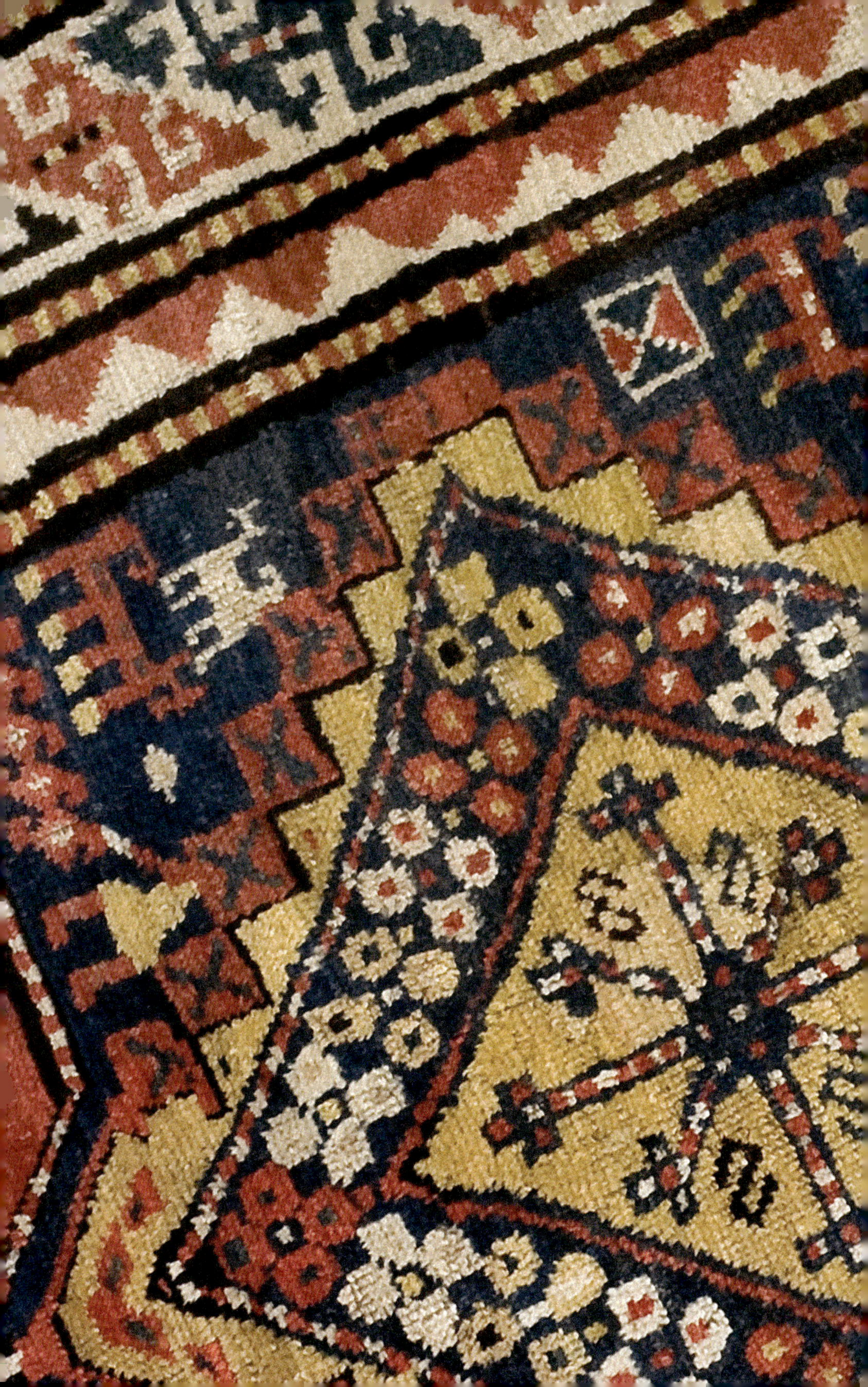

9. Moghan rug, Plains of Southeast Caucasus, Azerbaijan, 3rd quarter, 19th century

Wool-on-wool • 88 x 53 inches

In this rendering of the Memling gul format, the guls appear almost of secondary importance due to the presence of a dominant center medallion. The blue background triangles surrounding that medallion appear to tell a story of the weaver's life and environment as the figures in these triangles depict stylized humans and animals. This rug suggests a more primitive rendering of the Moghan gul format than the other examples. Its muted colors also set it apart. Rather than a Moghan, it may be an example of a rug by a nomadic weaver who picked up on the format and added her own flair with the medallion.

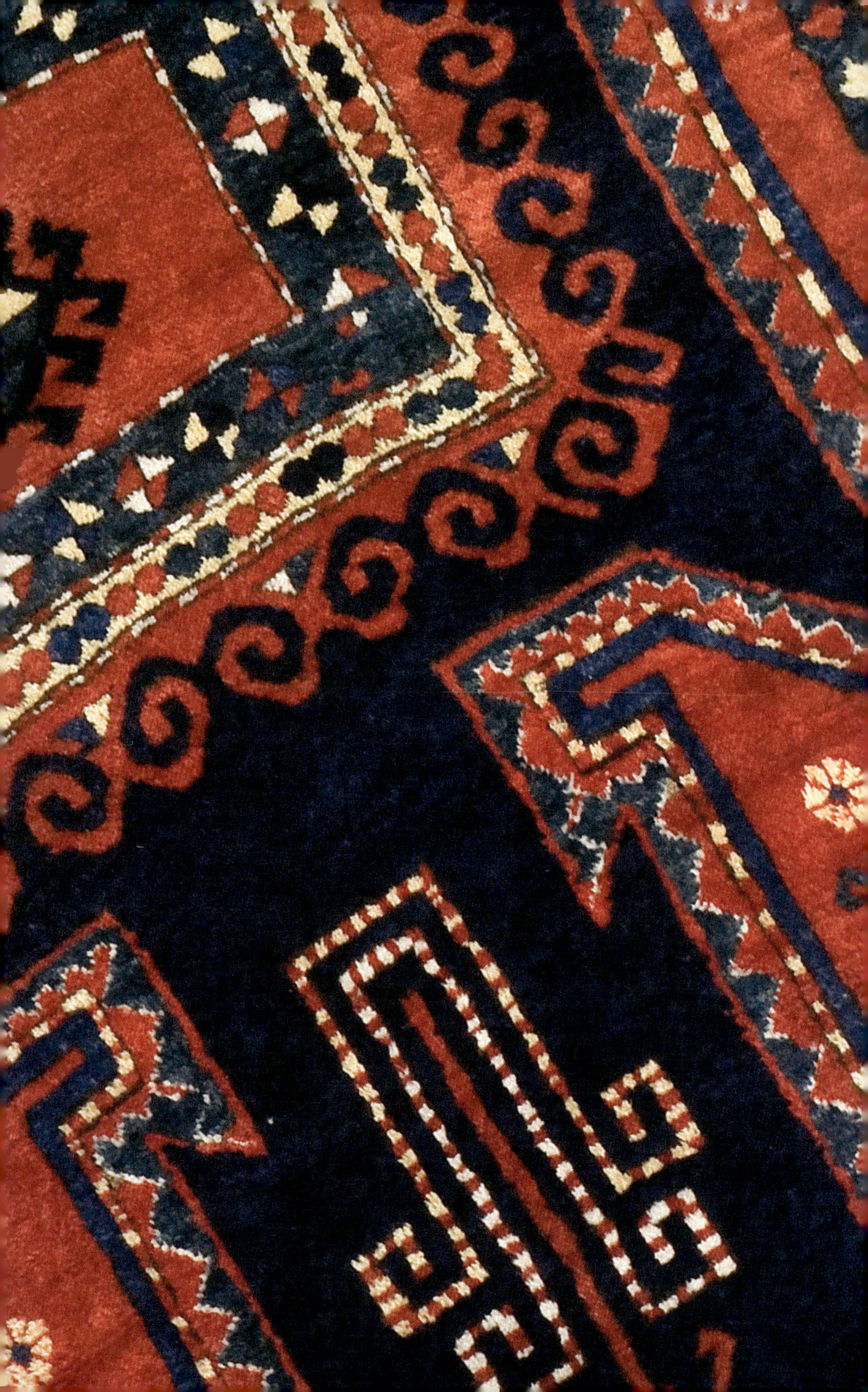

10. Sewan Kazak rug, West Caucasus, Armenia, 4th quarter, 19th century

Wool-on-wool • 83 x 57 inches

This rug is dominated by the central ornament known as the cruciform or Sewan cross, meaning it originated in or near the Armenian village of Sewan in the Lake Sewan area. In this rug, the dark-blue cruciform appears on a red field and with a squared-hexagon end. The design may suggest the outline of an Armenian church. This rug came out of Armenia around the time of the Soviet Union's collapse, when a large number of Armenians immigrated into Southern California. As such, this rug can be considered "Armenian-aged" compared to most other Kazaks of the type. The virtually original condition of this rug makes it appear younger and more recently woven than an "American-aged" rug.

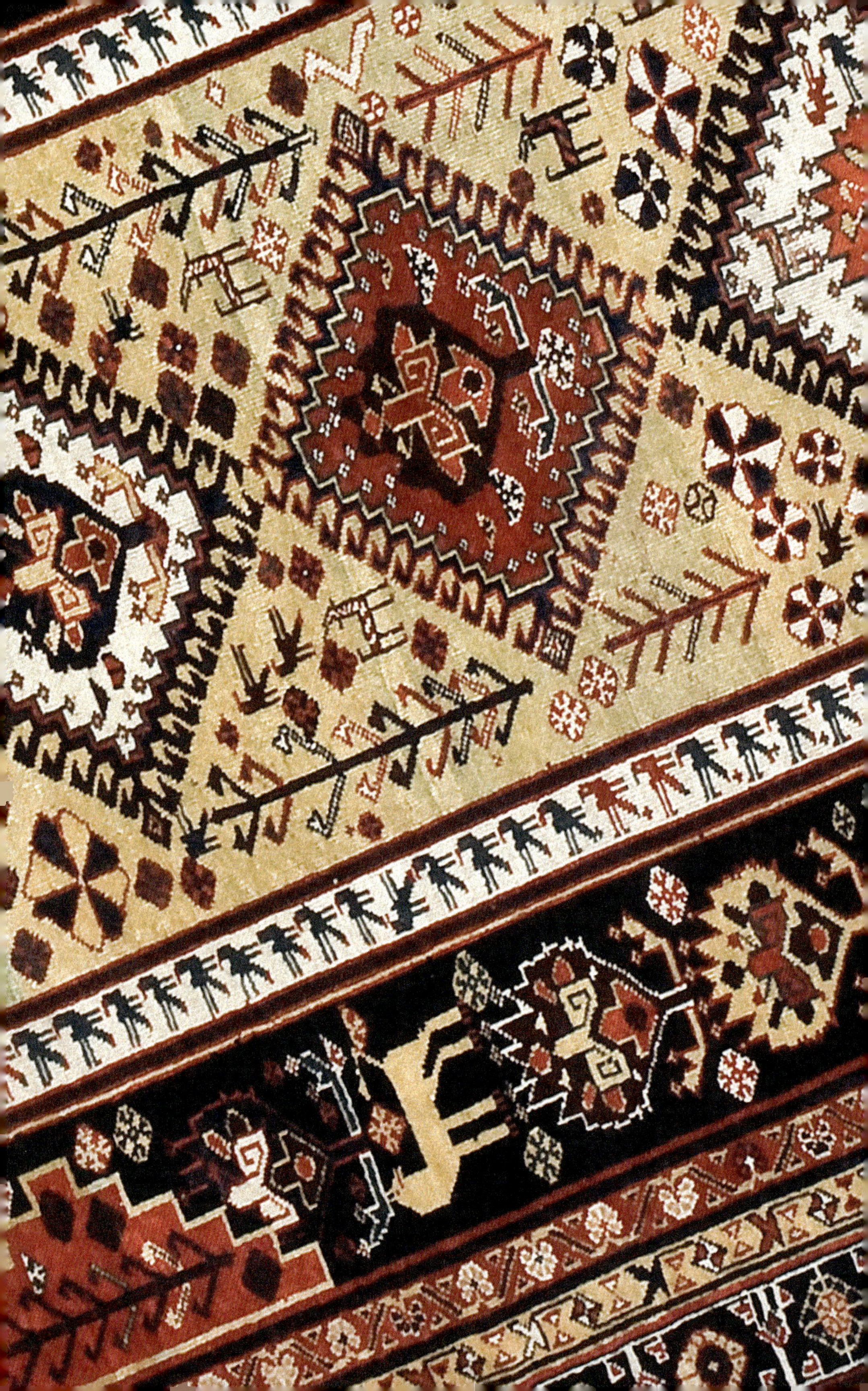

11. Qashqai rug, Southwest Persia, early 20th century

Wool-on-wool • 112 x 69 inches

The most distinguishing characteristic of this rug is that it features a "rug-within-a-rug," strikingly highlighted by the ivory border around the inner rug. This border contains a series of birds, one of which faces opposite to the others. It is likely this rug was not made on a whim but was woven for a special person or event. Originating from the Qashqai confederacy of Turkic tribes of southwest Persia, whose members were generally nomadic, the weaves and patterns of this type of rug were often fine and complexly detailed, not unlike some Caucasian rugs. The inner field has latch-hook medallions that are also found in some rugs from the Caucasus, and the birds in the inner border suggest comparison with catalogue number 5, which has

The field surrounding the smaller rug is filled with a series of shrub designs, three lions, and a variety of other figures. "Free-flowing" would be a good description of the rug. The orderliness and symmetry of the two large medallions and the spandrels is

---

WEAVERS planted innumerable little surprises throughout their rugs. . . . The random appearance of red birds is a surprise, as is the change of direction of one of the birds . . .

---

several large birds portrayed in different colors with plumes fully displayed. At a minimum, these design similarities convey the universality of design motifs employed by disparate rug groups. They may even suggest more direct connections, such as the migration of patterns from one region to another.

not disturbed by the abundance of other designs. James Opie illustrated this rug in his self-published book *Tribal Rugs of Southern Persia* (1981) and tentatively dates it as early 20th century.

Opie provided the following observations about this rug for this exhibition:

While Qashqai rugs are noted for both quality and variety, few examples compete with this remarkable piece on either count. Here, a master weaver has left her mark, embellishing a solid axis of symmetry with richly improvised details. Where do these details occur? Look at the stylized tree shape in the lower left spandrel. Look for the same tree in the spandrel on the lower right side. It isn't there, but the smaller "tree motifs" are. And so it continues throughout this rug, symmetry and improvisation, combined with uncommon freedom and skill. Describing this rug as a "rug-within-a-rug" only begins to tap the visual surprises to be encountered here.

In earlier comments about this rug, in the book noted above, Opie writes,

"Weavers planted innumerable little surprises throughout their rugs. Notice, for example, that the ivory border around the inner rug contains an unusual bird design, possible roosters. The random appearance of red birds is a surprise, as is the change of direction of one of the birds in the left-hand border. For another, there are three lions in the rug: one yellow lion on each side, and one ivory-colored between the top medallion and the inner rug. The space between the front and back legs of these animals is treated differently in each of the three forms."

Given its unusual and remarkable attributes, Opie suggested that the rug may have been woven for a special occasion or as a dowry object.

A NOTE ON THE MOUNTS

One of the tenets of professional textile conservation is "Do no harm." In practice, it translates as "Be the least invasive." In other words, do as little as possible to alter or diminish the original construction and composition of the textile. This precept should inform every aspect of the conservation process, from decisions about cleaning and stabilizing an object to considerations about its storage or display and approaches to museum exhibition.

Best exhibition practices are evident in Georgia Museum of Art's exhibition *Rugs of the Caucasus*. A fragile rug is best shown flat or at a slight angle and fully supported on a rigid mount. This method prevents strain on the weave structure, especially if the rug is large and/or heavy and there is no need to pin or stitch it in place. Rugs whose warps are strong enough to support the textile can be exhibited vertically, attached either to a large rigid wall mount or a wooden batten. The larger, heavier rugs in this exhibition are attached to battens using Velcro® hook and loop strips.

While the Velcro® system is an accepted best practice, more recently, conservators and preparators have discovered the utility of neodymium rare-

A FRAGILE RUG is best shown flat or at a slight angle and fully supported on a rigid mount. This method prevents strain on the weave structure, especially if the rug is large and/or heavy and there is no need to pin or stitch it in place.

earth magnets, lightweight and compact permanent magnets manufactured in a variety of strengths and sizes. Used with specially designed mounting boards and battens, the magnets are a safe and noninvasive alternative to Velcro® attachments, hand sewing, and pinning. Neodymium magnets have been used to support a number of rugs in this exhibition.

Kathleen Staples